I0814268

DISCOVERING THE UNITED STATES

Alaska

BY CHRISTA KELLY

Kids Core
An Imprint of Abdo Publishing
abdobooks.com

abdobooks.com

Printed in China.
052024
092024

Cover Photo: Shutterstock Images
Interior Photos: Bettmann/Getty Images, 4–5; Jacob Loyacano/Shutterstock Images, 7 (top left); Christine Kohler/iStockphoto, 7 (top right); LifeCollection Photography/Shutterstock Images, 7 (bottom left); iStockphoto, 7 (bottom right); Shutterstock Images, 9, 18, 23, 29 (bottom left), 29 (bottom right); Dominique Braud/Dembinsky Photo Associates/Alamy, 10; Michael Penn/The Juneau Empire/AP Images, 12–13; Alexandre Rosa/Shutterstock Images, 14, 28 (top left); Menno Schaefer/Shutterstock Images, 17; BriBar/E+/Getty Images, 20–21, 28 (bottom); Mint Images/Shutterstock Images, 25; Pep Roig/Alamy, 26; Red Line Editorial, 28 (top right), 29 (top)

Editor: Laura Stickney
Series Designer: Katharine Hale

Library of Congress Control Number: 2023949216

Publisher's Cataloging-in-Publication Data

Names: Kelly, Christa, author.
Title: Alaska / by Christa Kelly
Description: Minneapolis, Minnesota: Abdo Publishing, 2025 | Series: Discovering the United States | Includes online resources and index.
Identifiers: ISBN 9781098293727 (lib. bdg.) | ISBN 9798384912996 (ebook)
Subjects: LCSH: U.S. states--Juvenile literature. | Alaska--Juvenile literature. | Western States (U.S.)--Juvenile literature. | Physical geography--United States--Juvenile literature.
Classification: DDC 973--dc23

All population data taken from:
"Estimates of Population by Sex, Race, and Hispanic Origin: April 1, 2020 to July 1, 2022." *US Census Bureau, Population Division*, June 2023, census.gov.

CONTENTS

A group of miners pans for gold during the Klondike gold rush in the early 1900s.

The Klondike Gold Rush

It was August 1896. Shaaw Tláa, a Tlingit and Tagish Alaska Native woman, was hiking through the Klondike region of western Canada. Shaaw Tláa's brother and nephew walked alongside her. Her white husband joined them.

The group paused along Rabbit Creek. Suddenly, they spotted shimmering flecks at the river's bottom. Shaaw Tláa reached into the water and pulled out a gold nugget.

News of the group's discovery spread like wildfire. Over the next three years, more than 100,000 people traveled to the frozen land. They hoped to find gold and become rich. This event became known as the Klondike gold rush.

At first, the gold seekers lived in small mining camps. Most of them were located far away from civilization. Soon they started to create larger cities near the water. From those spots, people who found gold could transport it out of the area. Decades later, the land these miners settled would become the state of Alaska.

Alaska Facts

DATE OF STATEHOOD
January 3, 1959

CAPITAL
Juneau

POPULATION
733,583

AREA
665,384 square miles (1,723,337 sq km)

STATE BIRD

Willow ptarmigan

STATE TREE

Sitka spruce

STATE FLOWER

Alpine forget-me-not

STATE FISH

King salmon

Each US state has a different population, size, and capital city. States also have state symbols.

Alaska's Land

Alaska's southernmost point lies 500 miles (805 km) north of the rest of the United States. The state borders only Canada to the east.

The Arctic Ocean borders Alaska to the north. To the south and west is the Pacific Ocean.

Alaska has more land than any other US state. Almost half is made up of wetlands. Rainforests cover the southeastern coast. Fourteen mountain ranges stretch across Alaska too. Rivers include the Yukon River and the Kuskokwim River. Alaska also has forests

Glaciers

Alaska is known for its glaciers. Glaciers are big, tightly packed lumps of ice and snow. Over time, glaciers move. This shapes the land beneath them. There are more than 100,000 glaciers in Alaska.

The Brooks Range stretches for 700 miles (1,127 km) in northern Alaska and northern Canada.

and **tundra**. Much of the state is covered in ferns, mosses, and wildflowers.

More than 1,000 animal species live in Alaska. They include black bears, brown bears, polar bears, sheep, and goats. Whales, seals, and salmon swim in Alaskan waters.

The northern lights are caused by tiny particles that travel from the sun to Earth. Earth's magnetic field guides the particles toward the north pole where they collide with atoms to create colors.

Climate

Alaska has short spring and fall seasons. In winter, the state gets a lot of snow. In summer, the state is cool and rainy.

Some people call Alaska the Land of the Midnight Sun. It was given this nickname because the sun doesn't set during summer. In some parts of the state, the sun stays up for almost four months. This is because Alaska is very far north on the globe. During summer, Alaska is tilted toward the sun. During winter, it is tilted away from the sun. This means that in some areas, the sun doesn't rise for two months during winter. Alaska's **latitude** also allows people to see the northern lights.

Explore Online

Visit the website below. Does it give any new information about Alaska that wasn't in Chapter One?

Alaska Kids Corner

abdocorelibrary.com/discovering-alaska

A crowd gathers to welcome traditional canoes to Juneau, Alaska, as part of Celebration. This festival is observed by members of the Haida, Tlingit, and Tsimshian peoples.

CHAPTER 2

The People of Alaska

Historians believe American Indians arrived in Alaska more than 15,000 years ago. Native nations used **natural resources** to survive in the cold climate. The Ipiutak and Aleut nations built underground houses.

Tlingit totem poles are carved from cedar trees.

The Tlingit and Haida built houses with cedar planks and bark. To stay warm, Alaska Natives made clothes out of animal fur and skins.

In 1867, the US government bought the land from Russia for less than two cents per acre (0.4 ha). That's about 43 cents per acre in 2023. Many Americans believed Alaska's land was useless. But soon people found valuable gold and oil in the **territory**. People from all over the world came to Alaska to find jobs.

Today, 16 percent of Alaskans are Alaska Native or American Indian. There are more than 200 federally recognized native nations in Alaska. Many practice traditions of their **ancestors**, such as carving totem poles.

Sixty-four percent of Alaskans are white, 9 percent are Asian, and 8 percent are Hispanic or Latino. Four percent are Black.

Oil and tourism are major industries in Alaska. More than 2 million tourists visit each year. Many Alaskans work as tour guides and service workers. Fishing is another big industry. Seafood is one of Alaska's biggest trade products.

Airplanes in Alaska

Only 20 percent of Alaska is **accessible** by road. So some Alaskans rely on airplanes for everyday tasks, such as delivering mail and groceries. In 2023, 1 in 78 Alaskans had a pilot's license.

A group of fishermen clean salmon on a dock in Valdez, Alaska. More than 60,000 Alaskans work in the fishing industry.

Culture

One common activity in Alaska is dogsledding. The state's biggest dogsledding event is the world-famous Iditarod Trail Sled Dog Race.

A team of dogs starts the Iditarod Trail Sled Dog Race in Willow, Alaska.

Mushers drive sled dogs nearly 1,000 miles (1,600 km) from the town of Willow to Nome. This takes more than a week.

Food is also part of Alaskan culture. Many Alaskan dishes include salmon. Red king crab legs are also popular.

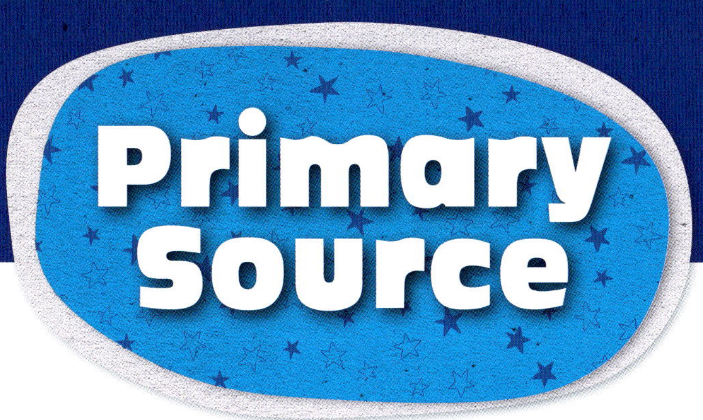

Sgwaayaans, also known as TJ Young, is a member of the Haida nation. He's been carving totem poles since he was 19 years old. He spoke about the importance of totem poles:

> You'd look at old totem poles back in the day [and] you'd be able to read them like a book. . . . They were documents. They documented a story or a family history.

Source: "Totem Pole Carving in Hydaburg, Southeast Alaska." *YouTube*, uploaded by Visit Southeast, 18 Aug. 2021, youtube.com. Accessed 28 Aug. 2023.

What's the Big Idea?

What is this quote's main idea? Explain how the main idea is supported by details.

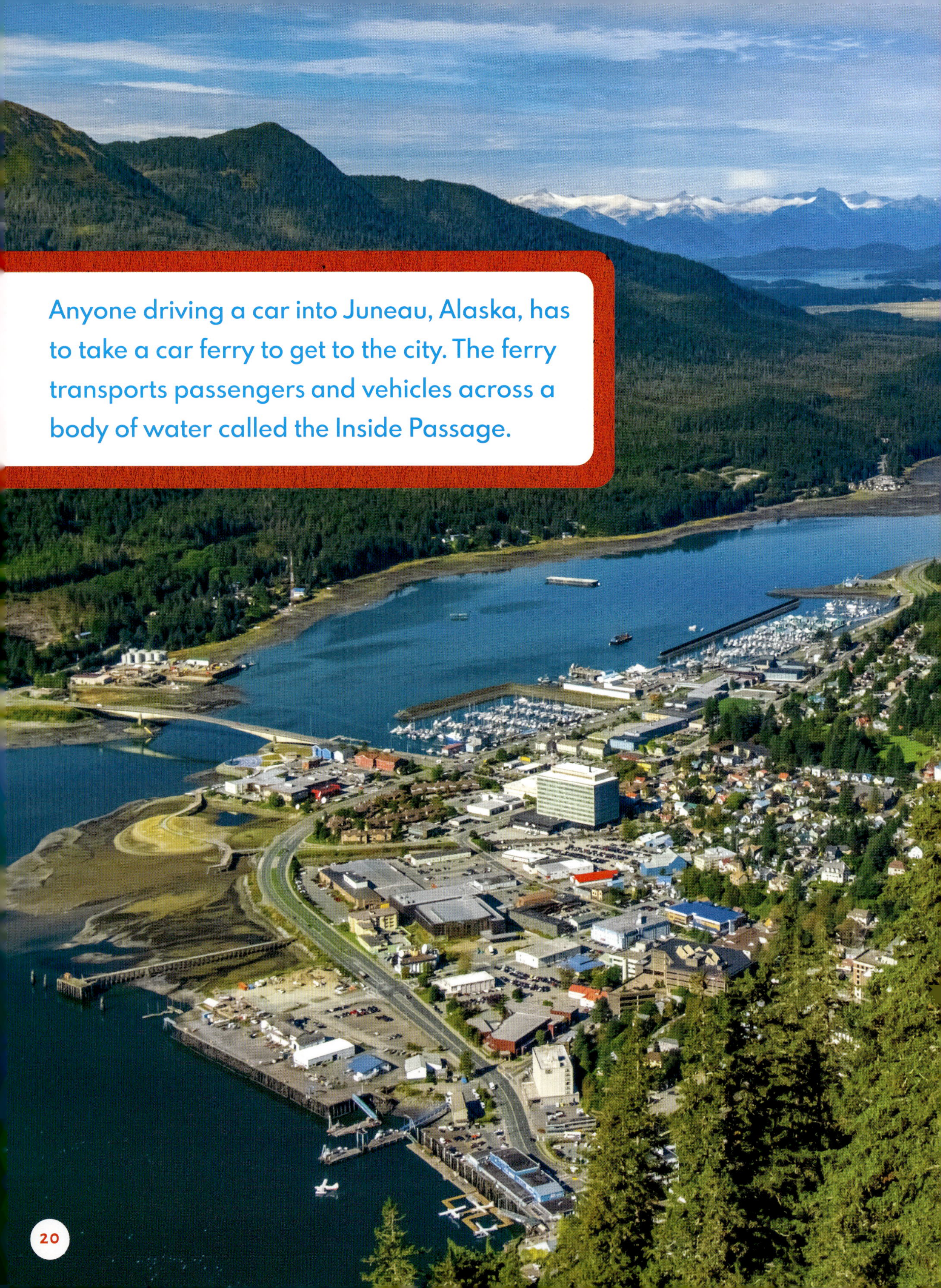

Anyone driving a car into Juneau, Alaska, has to take a car ferry to get to the city. The ferry transports passengers and vehicles across a body of water called the Inside Passage.

CHAPTER 3

Places in Alaska

The capital of Alaska is Juneau. It is located on the state's southeastern edge. Many people visit Juneau to go whale watching. Others visit to see the Mendenhall Glacier. It lies to the north and west of Juneau.

Anchorage is in southern Alaska. It is the most **populated** city in the state. People can visit the city's Alaska Native Heritage Center. Southeast of Anchorage is the town of Girdwood. This city is home to the Alaska Wildlife Conservation Center. Fairbanks is the second-largest city in Alaska by population. It is located in the center of the state.

Metlakatla Indian Community is located on an island in southern Alaska. It is the only Indian reservation in Alaska. Most residents are part of the Tsimshian nation.

Parks

Alaska has eight national parks. Denali National Park is one of the most popular. It's located in

Denali's peak is 20,310 feet (6,190 m) above sea level.

south-central Alaska. The park covers more than 6 million acres (2.4 million ha). It is home to Denali, the tallest mountain in North America.

Glacier Bay National Park and Preserve is located west of Juneau. The park features mountains and a temperate rainforest. Visitors can see wildlife and the Margerie Glacier.

Alaska also has several state parks. Chugach State Park is located near Anchorage. It has more than 280 miles (450 km) of trails.

Whale Watching

Whale-watching tours are popular in Alaska. Eight whale species live along Alaska's coasts. People commonly see humpback whales during whale-watching tours. About 10,000 humpback whales travel to Alaskan coasts every year.

Mountain Goats are a common sight in Glacier Bay National Park and Preserve.

Landmarks

Alaska has many landmarks. One is the Chilkoot Trail. It leads hikers along the path that miners walked during the Klondike gold rush.

Mount Redoubt is another important landmark. This active volcano is part of the Aleutian Range of mountains. Since 1900, the volcano has erupted several times. It is visible from the city of Kenai in southern Alaska.

The Chilkoot Pass is one of the most popular hiking spots in Alaska. Roughly 10,000 people hike it each day.

The Rainforest Sanctuary is located in Ketchikan. It features 40 acres (16 ha) of beautiful forest. Visitors can learn about native wildlife and plants. They might also catch a glimpse of black bears and brown bears!

People have called Alaska home for thousands of years. Today, the state has a rich history and culture. From glaciers to dogsledding races, Alaska has something for everyone to explore.

Further Evidence

Look at the website below, which talks about the Alaska Wildlife Conservation Center. Does it give any new evidence to support what you learned in Chapter Three?

Meet the Locals

abdocorelibrary.com/discovering-alaska

State Map

Tlingit Totem Pole

Juneau

Alaska: The Last Frontier

Arctic Ocean
RUSSIA
Utqiaġvik
BROOKS RANGE
Iditarod Trail Finish Line
Fairbanks
Yukon River
Denali
CANADA
Nome
Anchorage
Chugach State Park
Bering Sea
Kuskokwim River
Juneau
Kenai
Iliamna Lake
Mount Redoubt
Kenai Fjords National Park
Glacier Bay National Park
Chilkoot Trail
Becharof Lake
ALEUTIAN RANGE
Pacific Ocean
N
W
E
S

Denali

Kenai Fjords National Park

Glossary

accessible
able to be reached or entered into

ancestors
the people from whom a person is descended and who lived many generations ago

latitude
a location's distance north or south from Earth's equator

mushers
people who drive dogsleds

natural resources
materials found in nature that can be used by people

populated
settled or lived in

territory
a particular area of land that belongs to and is governed by a country

tundra
a flat, cold area of land without trees

Online Resources

To learn more about Alaska, visit our free resource websites below.

Visit **abdocorelibrary.com** or scan this QR code for free Common Core resources for teachers and students, including vetted activities, multimedia, and booklinks, for deeper subject comprehension.

Visit **abdobooklinks.com** or scan this QR code for free additional online weblinks for further learning. These links are routinely monitored and updated to provide the most current information available.

Learn More

Hanlon, Luke. *Iditarod Trail Invitational.* Abdo, 2024.

Payne, Stefanie. *The National Parks.* DK, 2020.

Tieck, Sarah. *Alaska.* Abdo, 2020.

Index

About the Author

Christa Kelly is an author and editor from Minnesota. She lives with her wife, Clare, and their two cats, Casey and Honey Cheddar. She visited Alaska in 2023. Her favorite part was seeing the wildlife.